Be Financially Responsible:
Five Simple Financial Roadmaps for Sustainable Life.

Alice A. Steve

INTRODUCTION

Imagine a peaceful night, a gleaming light, and the delicate stir of pages turning as you drench yourself in a book. Presently, picture an alternate scene: a jumbled work area, a heap of bills, and the mind-boggling weight of monetary vulnerability pushing down on you. Which situation would you rather encounter?

For some, the subsequent picture is nothing new—a steady battle with cash, obligations, and the subtle quest for monetary security. However, listen to this: it doesn't need to be like this. The excursion to independence from the rat race and manageability can start with a solitary step, and it begins on the spot with "Be Financially Responsible: Five Simple Financial Roadmaps for Sustainable Life."

The Night That Made a Huge Difference

Permit me to move you to a peaceful night in the relatively recent past. It was a night like any other, or so it appeared, as Sarah found a seat at her kitchen table with a heap of neglected charges, a decreasing bank balance, and a premonition in her chest. She was drained, focused, and, honestly, tired of the ceaseless pattern of monetary concerns.

As she gazed at the pile of envelopes, everyone holding a piece of her monetary riddle, Sarah couldn't resist the opportunity to contemplate whether there was a superior way. A method for assuming command over her funds, securing her future, and lastly, having the harmony of psyche she yearned for. Much to her dismay, this night would mark the start of her change—an excursion that would lead her to monetary obligation and supportability.

The Quest for Financial Freedom

Sarah's story isn't special. In a world immersed in monetary exhortation, a large number of us end up attempting to explore the intricacies of our monetary lives. We're assaulted with data about cash—how to acquire it, spend it, save it, contribute it, and plan for what's to come. However, in the midst of this racket of exhortation, we frequently feel unfastened and uncertain of which monetary choices to make and how to accomplish our objectives.

However, consider the possibility that I let you know that monetary obligations and manageability are conceivable as well as within your scope. Imagine a scenario in which I discovered that you hold the keys to your monetary prosperity and that all you want is the right guide to open the doors to a more brilliant, safer future.

This is exactly what "Be Financially Responsible" offers—an aid that engages you to assume command over your monetary predetermination, live economically, and break free from the pattern of monetary vulnerability.

The Path to Financial Obligation and Sustainability

In the accompanying sections, we will leave on an excursion together—an excursion that will divulge five straightforward yet strong monetary guides. Each guide is intended to address a particular feature of your monetary life, giving you the devices, information, and certainty expected to pursue informed choices and make a significant move.

As we set out on this excursion together, recall that you are in good company. Innumerable people, very much like you, are looking for a superior method for dealing with their funds, securing their prospects, and living additional satisfying lives. With "Be Financially Responsible" as your aide, you're prepared to transform your financial dreams into the real world.

Might it be said that you are prepared to venture out, to change your monetary life, and to break free from the chains of monetary vulnerability? Then we should start. The way to monetary obligation and supportability is anticipated, and it begins on the spot.

CHAPTER 1: Your Money Mindset: Understanding Your Beliefs in Money

Individuals acquire more from their folks and grandparents than from large feet, eye tone, self-control, energy for sports, or an imaginative twist. Most additionally accept their families' thoughts and mentalities towards money convictions, which are many times passed down from one age to another, alongside distant grandmother's blankets, familial photographs, and family culture. Grasping your cash convictions—your acquired family perspectives towards cash—can be the most important phase in working on your monetary choices and diminishing monetary pressure in your life.

Analysts refer to these acquired cash outlooks as "cash scripts." These are classifications of convictions related to dangerous monetary choices that create constant pressure.

A financial plan cannot be guaranteed to be incorrect, but it is not necessarily always correct either. Our contents are frequently slanted, overstated, or layered, comprising fragmented or incomplete bits of insight.

They are generally exceptionally relevant and valid in one situation, yet misleading in numerous others. Since our cash scripts are for the most part oblivious, we don't scrutinize their exactness or look at how much they are valid and work for us, yet we keep on following up on them as though they were altogether obvious.

Understanding the contents that underlie your monetary decisions might assist with further developing navigation and diminishing financial pressure.

The Four Variables Behind Your Cash Convictions

In a fascinating review, scientists at the College of Kansas analyzed four factors that envelop an assortment of cash scripts.

- Cash aversion: Some cash avoiders accept they don't have the right to have cash. Others think cash is terrible. One way or another, cash can be a wellspring of dread, nervousness, or revulsion. Cash avoiders frequently damage their monetary achievement. They might decide not to burn through cash on sensible and fundamental things, or they might part with cash, so they have as little as could be expected.

- Cash love: All cash admirers share a "conviction that more cash will tackle life's concerns and give joy." The prize of more cash turns into a carrot hanging just a little way off that is never fully reached. These convictions have been related to enthusiastic storage, absurd gamble-taking, betting, overspending, impulsive purchasing, and other disastrous monetary ways of behaving.

- Cash status: Individuals whose convictions show up on this level stick to the possibility that cash gives status. They see a reasonable qualification between financial classes, and their identity worth is frequently connected to total assets. What's more, status scripters generally liken accomplishment to cash. Some might profess to have more cash than they truly do to seem fruitful.

- Cash carefulness: The watchful accept that it means a lot to work and save. They are vigilant, parsimonious, and worried about funds. While these attributes can uphold sound monetary choices, the cautious are often restless about cash matters and careful about monetary gambles. Thus, their capacity to partake in the advantages and security of cash might be restricted.

Of the four, which variable or elements do you suppose underlie your cash scripts? Getting some margin to contemplate this can draw more attention to your cash ways of behaving.

Grasping Your Cash Convictions

Inside the four classifications, the following are ten cash scripts you could be telling yourself.

1. More cash will improve things. Families with this content might spend their lives collecting more to upgrade their lives or achieve optimal status.

2. Cash is terrible. Grounded in the conviction that cash makes individuals terrible or troubled, this content might prompt monetary destructive behavior.

3. I don't merit cash. This conviction might go with a legacy or bonus. It might likewise prompt individuals to procure underneath their true capacity.

4. I have the right to burn through cash. Indeed, everybody does; nonetheless,

when this prompts overspending, it creates monetary issues.

5. There is never sufficient cash. Dread and tension might make individuals work for extended periods, disregard connections, and neglect to partake in the advantages of their work.

6. There will always be sufficient cash. A conviction the universe will continuously give, regardless of whether an individual makes a move.

7. Cash is immaterial. This justification is used to pardon poor monetary choices.

8. Cash will give my life meaning. Individuals with this content frequently

right away and emphatically reject it. Their activities might recount an alternate story.

9. It's not pleasant or important to discuss cash. This mentality might be framed by the thought that it isn't acceptable to discuss cash, governmental issues, or religion.

10. If you are great, the universe will supply every one of your necessities. This conviction is common among individuals in aiding callings and those from solid, strict foundations.

1.1 Shifting Your Mindset: Improve Your Money Mindset

How you ponder cash can influence how you deal with your funds. Whenever you've recognized the variables behind your opinion on cash and you've analyzed the acquired cash scripts that impact your choices and conduct, you can start chipping away at working on your relationship with cash.

Many individuals who procure significant earnings and use wise judgment in different parts of their lives undermine their monetary security by pursuing poor monetary decisions. Now and again, acquired cash scripts are the issue.

The uplifting news is that it's feasible to meaningfully impact how you contemplate cash. In the first place, it's critical to recognize and comprehend the cash convictions that might be hindering your capacity to develop riches. The following stage is taking on better approaches to thinking, and that frequently implies getting familiar with cash.

Monetary information can be an incredible asset, particularly when you've accomplished the work to further develop how you ponder cash.

How can your convictions about cash affect your relationship with it?

Managing money is undeniable in a trade-driven world like our own.

Cash is quite possibly the most integral asset individuals connect with every day, whether they understand it or not.

The cash you acquire addresses work gives buying power, and has enormous scope for development and change.

For such a fundamental device, notwithstanding, cash frequently turns into a pessimistic power in individuals' lives.

Cash is both strong and disruptive.

Furthermore, with the general public progressively up to speed in commercialization, it's not shocking that many individuals have a terrible relationship with cash.

Those with loads of cash might use it rashly or find themselves incapable of getting a handle on more, while those with less may feel caught, frail, or angry at others.

Whether you have excessively or excessively little cash, it can be a critical stepping stone in your life.

Negative convictions about cash—and your relationship to it—can impact unfortunate spending and planning choices and lessen your feeling of happiness in your life.

To plan better, spend more astutely, and live more joyfully, you want to change your negative perspectives towards cash.

Assuming that you're keen on changing your relationship with your funds to improve things, do some spirit-looking and do whatever it takes to cure basic issues.

To begin, here are a few different ways you can effectively attempt to change your convictions about cash.

1. Recognize your cash contents.

The mentalities about cash shaped through youth encounters, parent stories, and battles keep on affecting individuals into adulthood.

These early-shaping perspectives and ways of behaving are called cash scripts, which have a lot to do with how you handle cash today.
Some cash scripts are sound. Others are not.

For instance, individuals who accept cash, show self-esteem, admire cash and material addition, or put down cash's significance are bound to have lower monetary results than the people who don't. Disengaging an issue is the most effective way to sort out some way to fix it, so on the off chance that you think your cash issues could emerge out of negative content, it's really smart to recognize it for what it is.

Since cash scripts are often framed in youth, finding out about the starting points of your perspectives towards cash by talking with your folks and family members about their attitudes is conceivable.

Notwithstanding, you can likewise find your cash script by counseling your memory to figure out where your convictions come from.

Whenever you've distinguished an issue, you can work without help from anyone else or with a monetary therapist to check negative idea examples and propensities.

2. Perceive social convictions towards cash

Like your family climate, your social climate can likewise impact your monetary mentalities.
In the US, they urge individuals to demolish their monetary contest to turn into "the best."
Since we frequently compare abundance with progress, this can leave individuals with humble financial balances feeling pointless about their accomplishments.

This isn't true all over the planet, nonetheless.
One author found, for instance, that the Swedish culture's prioritization of humbleness and congruity made monetary life more straightforward, even though the everyday costs were higher.
Cash is a piece of the way of life.

Hence, mentalities towards cash change all over the planet.

A few convictions are more grounded than others, and they all enjoy benefits and hindrances.

In any case, you can find out a lot about your relationship with cash by contrasting it with those in different nations.

At the point when you gain a more extensive perspective on monetary mentalities, you can get rid of the pieces of your convictions that aren't helping you.

3. Recall that money is an actual item.

Before web-based banking, cash was a device you could grasp—something actual that imparted value. Today, in any case, the singular worth of a dollar is frequently forgotten as we take a gander at our complete abundance as opposed to each piece of the entirety.

Perceive that cash is not a general given, but rather an instrument and framework embraced for comfort.

You ought to regard cash as an actual item rather than an emblematic thought, particularly if you need to quit conflating your total assets with your self-esteem.

On the off chance that you want an update that cash is a device, you could begin conveying bills again as opposed to depending on a charge or Visa.

Certain individuals additionally gather coins, which keeps the physical and, surprisingly, authentic parts of cash at the front of their brains.

By involving actual cash for little purchases, you can more readily perceive the influence of the cash you have while staying aware of how much cash you're spending.

4. Separate wants from needs.

Many individuals' disappointment with their monetary circumstances comes from the inclination that such a large number of things are far off.
Notwithstanding, a great many people who feel as such likely have to the point of accommodating their essential requirements, so the pressure and disappointment their disappointment causes them could cause them more damage than great.

Satisfaction and pay level are not straightforwardly related.
Bliss appears to level before yearly pay even reaches $100,000.
This demonstrates that cash truly can't purchase bliss.

Assuming you have to the point of fulfilling your necessities, you have to the point of being blissful.

The stunt for this situation is separating wants from needs.

Buyers are continually assaulted with messages letting them know they need either item to be content, famous, effective, cherished, and so forth.

To encourage a better relationship with cash, you should oppose these messages and characterize your necessities.

Be aware of the purposes for each purchase you make, and try not to substitute material products for a genuine answer for close-to-home issues.

5 Discuss your errors.

Many individuals feel disgraced about their monetary circumstances, particularly if they aren't as off as they would have expected to be.

As a result of this disgrace, individuals frequently try not to examine cash, no matter what, to keep themselves from looking clumsy.

This quietness is lamentable because it permits negative perspectives to putrefy and vices to carry on uncontrolled. Cash ought not to be something to be embarrassed about.

Talking transparently and truly about cash with your companions, friends, and family, or with an expert, can assist you in sorting out some way to work on your relationship with cash.

If you're bold, open up and talk about some cash botches.

CHAPTER 2: BUDGETING BASICS

Hardly any ideas are as central but as disregarded as budgeting. A term frequently summons pictures of perplexing calculation sheets, heaps of receipts, and the overwhelming errand of following each penny that streams all through your life. In any case, truly, budgeting isn't the foe of independence from the rat race; the compass guides you towards it. In this section, we'll leave on an excursion to demystify planning and divulge its actual power in forming your monetary fate.

Envision, briefly, that your monetary life resembles a boat heading out on the huge expanse of your objectives and dreams. Your financial plan is the navigational graph that guarantees you arrive at your ideal objective. Without it, you could float capriciously, trapped in the flows of motivational spending and unanticipated costs. With a very well-created financial plan, notwithstanding, you have a way forward, an arrangement that permits you to direct your monetary boat with reason and certainty.

At its center, planning revolves around one straightforward yet significant thought: living within your means. It's tied in with adjusting your spending to your pay, which leaves space for your monetary objectives and needs. Generally, it's the specialty of letting your cash know where to go as opposed to pondering where it went.

However, why, you could ask, is planning so significant? To respond to that inquiry, we should consider the narrative of Ella, a youthful expert with huge dreams and a check to coordinate. Ella had steady employment, an agreeable condo, and a public activity that kept her occupied. Life was sweet, or so it appeared.

Notwithstanding, as the months moved on, Ella started to see a disturbing theme.

Notwithstanding her apparently adequate pay, she wound up living check to check. The end of every month carried with it a feeling of fear as she battled to earn enough to get by. There was never sufficient cash to put something aside for her fantasy excursion, to square away her understudy loans, or to contribute to her future. The things she had buckled down for consistently appeared to be barely unattainable.

Ella's story isn't interesting. Large numbers of us have been there, trapped in a pattern of monetary pressure and vulnerability. Truly, without a financial plan, it's easy for your cash to get past you, passing you on with little to show for your diligent effort. A spending plan, notwithstanding, can break that cycle and put you in charge of your monetary fate.

In the pages that follow, we will investigate planning in its most straightforward structure, separating it into sensible advances that anybody can follow. You don't need to be a human calculator or a monetary master to make a spending plan that works for you. What you really do require is the readiness to assume responsibility for your monetary future and the obligation to stay on course.

We'll begin by assisting you with making an individual spending plan diagram that mirrors what is happening and your objectives. You'll figure out how to follow your costs with accuracy, acquiring knowledge of where your cash is truly going. We'll dive into the specialty of shrewd saving and investigate systems for overseeing and wiping out obligation, a significant stage on the way to independence from the rat race.

Planning isn't about limitation or hardship; it's about strengthening and opportunity. It's tied in with making deliberate decisions with your cash—decisions that line up with your qualities and goals. It's tied in with tracking down the harmony between getting a charge out of life today and getting your monetary prosperity tomorrow.

Your spending plan is your handy dandy guide and compass, directing you toward your monetary dreams. Thus, we should head out on this journey of disclosure, equipped with the information and instruments to make our monetary desires a reality.

2.1 Creating a Budget

A financial plan is only an arrangement. It's anything but a limitation on spending—it's an arrangement for how you'll manage your cash. It's an arrangement for what's coming in and what's going out.

At the point when you figure out how to make a spending plan and do it consistently, you're giving your cash motivation. You're assuming command. Farewell, cash nervousness. Hi, cash objectives.

A great many people need some approach to seeing where their cash is going every month. A financial plan can assist you with feeling more in charge of your funds and make it simpler to set aside cash for your objectives. Try to figure out a method for following your funds that works for you.

Making a financial plan is an extraordinary method for following where your cash goes every month and a significant stage in setting your funds up. A spending plan can make it more straightforward for you to accomplish monetary achievements, for example, constructing a secret stash or putting something aside for an initial installment on a home.

While the errand might appear to be overwhelming, making a budget is not unreasonably troublesome. Additionally, once you have one, the majority of the work is finished, and you can make minor changes to your ways of managing money or pay change. There are numerous sites and planning applications that you can use to get everything rolling, or you can make your calculation sheet.

The following is how to make a financial plan utilizing a calculation sheet, yet a large number of the means are equivalent to other planning techniques. Go ahead and get innovative with it—you can download formats online through Google Sheets, MS Excel, and different destinations or build one creatively by yourself. This is the way to make a financial plan in five stages.

- **Ascertain your net gain.**

The initial step is to figure out how much cash you make every month. You'll need to ascertain your overall gain, which is how much cash you acquire with fewer charges.

If you get a standard check from your boss, notwithstanding whether you're part-time or full-time, the sum recorded is possibly your total compensation.

You will need to take away those derivations to ensure you have an unmistakable image of your salary.

On the off chance that you are independent, are independently employed, or don't get a normal check, you'll have to deduct charges from your pay sum. The independent work charge rate is 15.3%, as indicated by the IRS. You can utilize this TaxAct mini-computer to gauge how much duty you're expected to pay in a year. Then, at that point, you can separate by 12 to get a month-to-month gauge.

- **List month-to-month expenses.**

Ten, you'll need to assemble a rundown of your month-to-month expenses.
Here are a few normal costs:

Food

Telephone, web, link, and month-to-month streaming membership
Recreation center participation
Kid care
Credit installments (like understudy, auto, and individual)
Utilities (like power, water, and gas)
Lease or home loan installments
Transportation (for example, gas, train tickets, and transport admissions)
Family products
Travel
Being insured (like wellbeing, home, and auto)
Others may include, for example, gifts, diversion, and clothing.

It's likewise great to remember subtleties for the amount you're saving every month, whether that is into customary or high-return investment accounts or an individual retirement account, like a Roth IRA.

- **Mark fixed and variable costs**

Whenever you've incorporated a rundown of your month-to-month expenses, mark whether they're fixed or variable. Fixed costs are bills you can't stay away from utilities, transportation, protection, food, and obligation reimbursement. Variable costs will generally be more adaptable—your rec center participation, for example, or the amount you spend on eating out.

If cash was tight, you could constantly drop your exercise center enrollment and abridge your feasting-out spending; however, you are logically continuously required to pay a compensation lease or your home loan.

- **State your monthly cost for every expense.**

After you separate fixed and variable costs, list the amount you spend on each cost each month. You can look into your spending and financial records.

Fixed costs are easier to list on your spending plan than variable costs since the expense is, for the most part, very month-to-month. For instance, obligation reimbursement on a home loan or vehicle credit will cost a similar amount every month. Yet, fixed utilities, like electricity and gas, and variable expenses, like eating and family merchandise, frequently vary month-to-month, so you'll have to do the math to view them as normal.

For these classifications and any place your spending changes from month to month, decide the typical month-to-month cost by checking out 3 months' worth of expenditure. To work out the normal sum you spend on food, for instance, include all of your staple spending during the past 90 days and divide the gap by three.

Assuming you find that the typical amount you spend on regular food items every month is $375, you might need to gather together and put forth the spending line of $400.

- **Adjust and adapt.**

The last move towards making a spending plan is to contrast your net gain with your month-to-month expenses. Assuming you notice that your costs are higher than your pay, you'll have to make a few changes.

For example, suppose your costs cost $300 more than your month-to-month net compensation. You ought to survey your variable costs to track down ways of reducing expenses by $300. This might incorporate reexamining the amount you spend on food, family products, streaming memberships, and other adaptable expenses.

It's really smart to lessen these expenses and consistently make changes in how much cash you spend so you can keep away from obligations.

Then again, assuming you have more pay after posting your costs, you can expand specific regions of your financial plan. Preferably, you'd utilize this additional cash to build your investment funds, particularly if you don't have a just-in-case account. Yet, you could likewise utilize the cash on trivial things like feasting or voyaging.

On the off chance that you still need to get a high-return bank account, think about opening one, like Marcus by Goldman Sachs High-Return Online Reserve funds, and procuring multiple times more revenue than customary records.

- **Subsequent stages**

After you make a financial plan, the next step is to adhere to it. You can consider yourself responsible in various ways. First off, you can set up updates with your charge card and financial balances when you arrive at a preset spending sum. You should likewise have a go at following every one of your costs into your calculation sheet or planning application after you make a purchase. Furthermore, assuming you share costs with another person, ensure you're both in total agreement with the financial plan and keep each other on target.

Importance of Budget

Making a spending plan could sound overwhelming; however, a clear cycle starts with grasping your monetary situation. The initial step is to accumulate data about your pay, costs, obligations, and monetary objectives.

Consider this gathering the bits of a riddle. When you have every one of the pieces, you can see the master plan and start making your financial plan outline.

Your spending plan ought to be an impression of your remarkable conditions, requirements, and yearnings. It's anything but a one-size-fits-all format, yet a customized monetary arrangement. There's really no need to focus on hardship except for pursuing decisions aligned with your needs.

Consider briefly what a spending plan can mean for different parts of your monetary life:

1. Monetary Lucidity: A spending plan gives an unmistakable depiction of your monetary circumstances. It resembles turning on a light in a dim room and uncovering all your pay sources, costs, obligations, and reserve funds. This lucidity permits you to come to informed conclusions about where to allot your assets.

2. Command Over Spending: Without a financial plan, letting your spending completely go is simple. You could surrender to incautious buys, buy into administrations you don't require, or feast out unreasonably. A spending plan reigns in these propensities by drawing certain lines and needs.

3. Crisis Readiness: Life is flighty, and surprising costs can mess up your monetary soundness. A good-to-go spending plan incorporates a backup stash classification, guaranteeing that you're prepared to deal with

unanticipated difficulties without wrecking your monetary objectives.

4. Sorting out Debt: In the event that you have debts to sort out, a spending plan is your partner in handling them. It assists you with distributing additional assets towards obligation reimbursement and speeds up your journey to becoming obligation-free.

5. Putting something aside for What's to come: Whether you long for homeownership, retirement, or going into business, a financial plan empowers you to save reliably for these drawn-out goals. It changes these fantasies into significant monetary plans.

6. Diminishing Monetary Pressure: Monetary pressure is a typical present-day illness. It can influence your prosperity, connections, and, surprisingly, your actual well-being. A financial plan gives you true serenity by providing you with a feeling of control and a way forward.

7. Accomplishing Monetary Objectives: Past overseeing everyday costs, a spending plan assists you with dispensing assets for your objectives. Need to venture to the far corners of the planet, send your children to school, or resign easily? Your spending plan is your guide to arriving.

2.2 Saving and Managing Debt

Being indebted is normally depicted as a monetary privilege that ties individuals to an existence of stress and restlessness.
All organizations, from little new companies to huge partnerships, have their own portion of monetary liabilities. Yet, what frequently recognizes a fruitful and beneficial association is the means by which it manages its obligations.

This is where the board plans come in. Otherwise called DMP, this plan offers an obligation-rebuilding arrangement that permits entrepreneurs to gradually settle their liabilities without devastating organizational income. Likewise, a decent executive plan offers many advantages that entrepreneurs can appreciate.

Here are viable methodologies for adjusting monetary commitments while making every second count.

Change your discernment about debts.

The most important phase in overseeing debt while maintaining an exciting and satisfying life is to change your outlook. View obligation as a brief stage, a necessary evil, instead of a weight that characterizes your reality. Regardless of how terrible it appears, you can always carry on with a decent life while taking care of your obligations.

Further, develop your cost arrangement.

The next stage to take is to distribute a part of your profit to clear your obligations while saving a little cash for entertainment exercises and encounters. A very well-created financial plan is the groundwork for fruitful obligations and pleasant living. Track your pay and costs perseveringly, and focus on obligation reimbursement in your month-to-month spending plan.

Try not to maintain an unsustainable lifestyle.

You can't be underwater and carry on with an extravagant way of life. Although living economically doesn't expect you to quit any pretense of all that fulfills you, you should search for practical options for diversion, eating, and relaxation exercises. Search for nothing or minimal-cost occasions, take strolls, or plan home bases with your companions. Partaking in minimal-cost or free exercises won't just assist you with dealing with your obligations; they will likewise give you new encounters and associations.

Center on high-loan costs

Assuming that you have different obligations, focus on taking care of those with higher loan fees first. By handling exorbitant premium obligations early, you'll get a good deal on interest installments and speed up your way to the obligation opportunity.

Arrange an adaptable installment plan with your leasers

Make it a point to put an adaptable installment plan in place if you're confronting monetary difficulties. Numerous lenders will figure out elective installment plans or even settle for not exactly everything owed. Impart straightforwardly and genuinely to track down a commonly valuable arrangement.

Construct a just-in-case account

While overseeing obligations is fundamental, don't disregard assembling a secret stash. Having a well-being net for unforeseen costs will keep you from falling further into obligation during testing times.

Kill late installment punishments

Besides chopping down loan costs, utilizing an obligation to the board plan can likewise assist you with disposing of punishment expenses. Your acknowledged instructor can haggle with your lenders and persuade them to postpone any extra charges put on you because of late or missed installments. Along these lines, you can zero in on paying the sum that you owe and escape obligation quickly.

Look for Proficient Monetary Counsel

Assuming that you wind up attempting to oversee obligations or are uncertain of the best methodology, consider looking for direction from a monetary guide or somebody who is learned around there. They can give you custom-fitted procedures and assist you with keeping focused on independence from the rat race.

CHAPTER 3: Investing for the Future

It is a lot simpler and more charming to take the pay, the cash we have procured and endeavored to get, and burn through every last bit of it consistently—buying anything we desire and not pondering what's to come. The issue, concerning cash, is that we basically aren't organizing and dealing with enough.

That is a pity since there are such endless inspirations to set something aside for what the future holds. The future doesn't just mean retirement; what's to come is tomorrow. Saving means allowing a break from the check to really take a look at a cycle or taking into account a significant purchase not excessively far off, like a vehicle, journey, or house. Living check-to-check, shockingly, isn't simply something that happens to those procuring lower earnings, but to anybody unfit to make a financial plan and follow it, notwithstanding making investment fund objectives and contacting them.

Between today and the end of our pay procurement days, a tonne can and will occur. We could lose our job(s), take a boost in salary or lessen it, move, or become unfit to work. Planning about the pay we make now to devise plans for what's in store is quite possibly everything we can manage with our well-deserved cash.

Assuming command over your cash through powerful future speculations is the way to partake in a tranquil life. You might not have six-figure compensation, yet all you really want to lay out for a brilliant future is to turn into a savvy cash saver and financial backer. Monetary planning isn't tied in with saving pennies or concocting convoluted spending plans; you simply need the proper venture portfolio to gather cash over the long run.

Mechanize investment funds so the cash stays. Assuming you hold on for the rest of the month to save, the probability will be that there isn't much to pass on to save. Make it programmed and have cash stored straight out of your check, or have a piece go into a bank account at whatever point you put aside an installment. On the off chance that you have a couple of reserve fund targets, you can follow the cash you put into each record and put it through one record or use at least one or two investment accounts open for different objectives. At the point when you see your reserve funds' development, you are bound to keep them there.

Numerous financial backers watched their portfolios decline the year before. Maybe you were one of them, but it won't matter if that's the case in 2023. That is on the grounds that when you contribute as long as possible, the transient decay becomes less significant.

In any case, that never implies going ahead despite any potential risks. With the vulnerability that actually holds the monetary business sectors, it means quite a bit to choose the right blend of speculations to expand development in your portfolio.

The following are nine non-convoluted tips to assist you with making shrewd future speculations and making riches.

- Start early.

Start effective financial planning with even a modest quantity of cash as you begin procuring. Future ventures of even a modest quantity from the get-go can impact your future personal satisfaction.

- Contribute for as long as possible.

There is no handy solution for development. To rake in boatloads of cash, you should contribute purposefully and reliably over the long run. This is one of the main strides towards building a steady future money growth strategy.

- Grasp your prerequisites.

Decide on your prerequisites and objectives prior to making a choice. Long-haul future ventures are required for necessities like your youngster's schooling or your retirement. Buying a home or a vehicle will require a transient venture. Be that as it may, be functional in your methodology.

- Decide your gambling resistance.

Before you start your future venture, decide how much risk you will confront and your ability to rest serenely during unstable business sectors, and gap your assets across a few speculation roads.

- Contribute to charge motivations

While assessing charge-advantaged future money growth strategies, select a choice where the sum you get on development is likewise tax-exempt, like life insurance. This benefit is likewise accessible for an assortment of future speculation items and installments. In any case, tax cuts are as per charge regulations that are likely to change.

- Focus on resource distribution

It's incredibly challenging to estimate which stocks or finances will succeed over many years. The best strategy is to put resources into an expansive assortment of values and securities reserves that compare to your gamble resilience and can possibly give predominant long-haul returns.

- Pick new assets with an alert

Consider another asset offering, provided that it has anything particular to offer and assuming it praises your current ventures.

- Contribute during a drop.

Put resources in a purposeful way consistently, and if conceivable, throughout a fall.

- Be industrious for abundance creation, contributing.

Be a supported financial backer, selling just when you truly need assets or when anything appears to be significantly amiss with your resources.

Picking the right extra security plan not only safeguards the fate of your friends and family but can likewise function as a monetary instrument. The thought is to choose money growth strategies that are safe for your future as well as prove useful in the event of a horrible circumstance.

Putting resources into a life coverage strategy permits you to guarantee an agreeable and deferential life for your precious ones even after you're no longer there to give it yourself. A disaster protection strategy gives the truly necessary monetary support to the group of policyholders in the event of their less-than-ideal downfall. This assists the family with keeping up with their way of life even without the sole provider.

Besides this, an extra security strategy likewise offers noteworthy back with negligible dangers. This is the very thing that makes disaster protection approaches one of the most pursued and shrewd future speculation devices that anyone could hope to find on the lookout.
Notwithstanding, prior to putting resources into a disaster protection strategy, investigating the different accessible choices and picking an

arrangement that suits the prerequisites of your family and your monetary goals is significant.

Key Focus Points

Saving adequately for the future—characterized as one or the other tomorrow or thirty years from now—is significant.

Key stages for saving incorporate making a spending plan (with a live-in accomplice in the event that you make them survey), your costs, and understanding your family's income.
Other key advances incorporate robotizing your reserve funds, searching for ways of conserving by recognizing needs and setting a model for youngsters.
Make sure to work on a periodic lavish expenditure.
The best opportunity to begin saving? At this moment,

Explicit Strides for Saving

When you understand the significance of saving and the role that it plays in your day-to-day existence, making objectives is the next stage to keeping focused. Part of defining monetary objectives is ensuring you can meet them. You can utilize a web-based reserve fund number cruncher, for instance, to ensure your necessities line up with your arrangement.

Equipped with the schooling and apparatuses to make sensible objectives for your cash, the time has come to find and commit the cash to arrive at your objectives.

3.1 Amassing Wealth Over Time

Creating financial momentum is an objective that many individuals desire; however, it can frequently appear to be a mind-boggling task. It requires investment, exertion, and training to find lasting success with this objective, so don't be tricked by pyramid schemes and unrealistic open doors that can send you down a perilous path.

Fortunately, there are standards and systems that can help anybody create and save financial stability over the long haul. What's more, the sooner you begin trying these, the better your odds of coming out on top.

Underneath, we have framed a few critical standards for creating financial stability, including laying out objectives and fostering an arrangement, putting resources into training and abilities, overseeing obligations, saving and effective money management, safeguarding your resources, grasping the effect of duties, and building areas of strength for a set of experiences. In this article, we will investigate every one of these standards and how they can assist you with accomplishing your monetary objectives.

Key Action Points

Creating financial well-being over the long haul involves following three essential advances and adhering to them.
The initial step is to bring in sufficient cash to cover your fundamental requirements, with some leftovers for saving.

The subsequent step is to deal with your spending so you can expand your reserve funds.
The third step is to put your cash in a wide range of resources so that it's appropriately differentiated for the long stretch.

1. Bring in cash.
The principal thing you really want to do is begin bringing in cash. This step might appear to be rudimentary, but it is the most essential one for people who are just beginning. You've most likely seen graphs showing that a limited quantity of cash consistently saved and permitted to intensify over the long run can eventually develop into a significant total. Be that as it may, those diagrams never answer this

fundamental inquiry: How would you get cash to save in any case?

There are two essential approaches to bringing in cash: through acquired pay or automated revenue. Procured pay comes from how you make ends meet, while automated revenue is gotten from ventures. You might not have any recurring, automated revenue until you've brought in sufficient cash to start financial planning.

In the event that you are either going to begin a vocation or considering a profession change, these inquiries might assist you with settling on what you believe you should do—and where your procured pay will come from:

What do you appreciate? You will perform better, form a more drawn-out, enduring vocation, and be bound to succeed monetarily by accomplishing something that you appreciate and view as significant. Truth be told, one investigation discovered that in excess of nine, out of 10 specialists said they would exchange a level of their lifetime profit for more prominent significance at work.

What are you great at? Take a gander at how you get along nicely and how you can utilize those gifts to make money.
What will compensate fairly? See vocations utilizing what you appreciate and do well that will measure up to your monetary assumptions.

How would you arrive? Find out about the schooling, preparation, and experience necessities expected to seek after your chosen profession choices.
Considering these contemplations can assist with putting you on the right path.
An effective method for boosting your potential is to put resources into your schooling, that is, the acquisition of more knowledge and abilities. Earning progressed scholastic college educations, industry-explicit accreditations, and preparing programs are valuable to assembling your human resources.

2. Put forth objectives and foster an arrangement.

Why will you utilize your abundance? Would you like to finance your retirement—perhaps an exit from any 9-to-5 work? Pay for your children to attend a university? Purchase a subsequent home. Give your abundance to a good cause. Defining objectives is a fundamental initial phase in creating financial stability. At the point when you have a reasonable vision of what you need to accomplish, you can make an arrangement that will assist you in arriving.

Begin by characterizing your monetary objectives, like putting something aside for retirement, purchasing a home, or taking care of obligations. Be explicit about how much cash you really want to accomplish every objective and the time span in which you desire to accomplish it.

Whenever you have defined your objectives, you ought to foster an arrangement for accomplishing them. This might include making a spending plan to assist you with setting aside more cash, expanding your pay through schooling or professional success, or putting resources into resources that will see their worth over an extended period of time. Your arrangement ought to be sensible, adaptable, and zeroed in on the long haul. Consistently survey your headway and make changes depending on the situation to keep yourself on target.

3. Set aside cash.

Just bringing in cash won't assist you with creating financial momentum, assuming you wind up spending everything. In addition, in the event that you need more cash, set something aside for your close-term commitments (like bills, a lease, or a home loan) or for a crisis. You ought to focus on saving enough, regardless of anything else. Numerous specialists suggest having months' (e.g., three to six) worth of pay set aside for such circumstances.

To save more cash for creating financial stability, think about these moves:

Track your spending for, basically, a month. You should utilize a monetary programming bundle to assist you with doing this; however, a little pocket-size journal could likewise get the job done. Record all your consumptions, regardless of how little; many individuals are astonished to see where all their cash goes.

Track down the fat and trim it. Separate your consumption into requirements and needs. Food, a safe house, and apparel are clear necessities. Add medical coverage charges to that rundown, alongside collision protection assuming that you own a vehicle, and extra security assuming that others are reliant upon your pay. Numerous different consumptions will simply be needed.

Put forth a reserve fund objective. Try to stick to it until you have a realistic idea of how much money you can save each month. This doesn't imply that you need to live like a penny pincher or be economical constantly. On the off chance that you're meeting your reserve fund objectives, go ahead and reward yourself and go overboard (with a suitable sum) on occasion. You'll feel significantly improved and be inspired to keep on track.

Put saving money into programming. One simple method for saving a limited sum every month is to arrange with your manager or bank to naturally move a specific piece of each and every check into a different reserve fund or venture account. Essentially, you can put something aside for retirement by having cash naturally removed from your compensation and put into your boss's own or comparable arrangement. Monetary organizers normally encourage contributing to some extent to get your manager's full matching commitment.

Track down high-return investment funds. Boost the result of your investment funds by looking for bank accounts that have the highest loan costs and the lowest expenses.
Remember this, as well: You can unfortunately cut a limited amount of costs. If your expenses

are as of now down deep, you ought to investigate ways of expanding your pay.

One of the most incredible ways to be certain you are saving enough is to set up a spending financial plan. Scale back overabundance and pointless spending, and put that cash in the bank, all things being equal

4. Save

Whenever you've figured out how to save some cash, the next stage is financial planning, so it will develop. The cash put in reserve funds is significant, yet the loan costs attributed to store accounts will generally be exceptionally low, and your money will lose buying control after some time to expansion.

Maybe the main money management idea for novices (or any financial backer, besides) is enhancement. Your objective ought to be to spread your cash among various sorts of ventures. That is on the grounds that speculations perform diversely at various times. For instance, in the event that the financial exchange is on a terrible streak, bonds might be giving great returns. Or, on the other hand, if Stock C is struggling, Stock D might be on a tear.

Shared reserves give some underlying broadening since they put resources into a wide range of protections. What's more, you'll accomplish more prominent expansion on the off chance that you put resources into both a stock asset and a security store (or a few stock assets and a few security assets), for instance, as opposed to only either.

As another overall principle, the more youthful you are, the more risk you can stand to take since you'll have more years to compensate for any misfortunes.

Sorts of speculations

Ventures change concerning hazards and are likely to return. When in doubt, the more secure they are, the lower their possible return, as well as the other way around.

On the off chance that you're not currently acquainted with the different kinds of speculations, it merits investing a little energy in looking into them. While there is a wide range of intriguing ventures, the vast majority will need to begin with the rudiments: stocks, securities, and common assets.

Stocks are portions of possession in an organization. At the point when you purchase stock, you own a small cut of that organization and will profit from any ascent in its portion cost as well as any profits that it pays out. Stocks are by and large considered less secure than bonds, yet stocks can likewise differ broadly in risk, starting with one enterprise and then moving on to the next.

Bonds are like IOUs from an organization or government. At the point when you purchase a security, the guarantor vows to take care of your cash, with a premium, after a specific period. As an extremely general guideline, bonds are thought of as safer than stocks, yet with less expected potential gain. Simultaneously, a few bonds are more hazardous than others; bond-rating organizations allot them letter grades to mirror that.

Shared reserves are pools of protections—frequently stocks, bonds, or a mix of the two. At the point when you purchase common asset shares, you get a cut of the whole pool. Shared reserves additionally change in risk, contingent upon what they put resources into.

Before you begin the investment of your money, ensure you have adequate reserve funds and some cash put away to deal with any startling monetary crises.

5. Make sure your asset is safe.

You've endeavored to bring in your cash and develop your abundance. The most terrible thing could be to lose everything because of an unexpected misfortune or unanticipated occasion. A fire can torch your home, a fender bender can cause harm and hospital expenses, or an unexpected passing can mean a deficiency of future pay.

Protection is a critical piece of creating your financial momentum since it gives you insurance from these and other perils. Home protection will supplant your home and possessions in the event of a fire, accident coverage will make you entire after an auto crash, and extra security will pay your recipients a passing advantage on account of an unfavorable demise. Long-haul handicap insurance is one more sort of contract that will supplant your pay assuming you become harmed, sick, or generally weakened and unfit to work. Indeed, even young, sound individuals ought to consider protection items since they will quite often turn out to be more costly as you get older. That implies that regardless of whether you are 26 years of age and single, purchasing life coverage could be much more practical than when you are 10 years older and have an accomplice, kids, and a home loan.

6. Limit the effect of charges.

Charges are a frequently neglected delay in your growing, strong financial foundation endeavors. Obviously, we are dependent upon personal duty and deals as we bring in and spend cash; however, our speculations and resources can likewise be burdened. That is why it is fundamental to grasp your expense openings and foster techniques to limit their effect.

One more procedure for limiting charges is to be aware of the timing and area of your ventures. By holding speculations for more than a year, you can exploit the lower long-haul capital increase charge rate, which is by and large lower than the transient capital increase duty and personal expense rates. You ought to likewise be aware of where certain resources are held. Given the decision, a pay-delivering resource like a profit-paying stock or corporate security ought to be put in a duty-advantaged account where these installments won't set off available occasions. A development stock that will just create capital additions (as opposed to paying) could rather be better situated in an available record.

Working with a certified expense professional, like a bookkeeper or a guaranteed public bookkeeper, can assist you with keeping steady over these progressions and foster a duty methodology that works for your particular monetary circumstance. By understanding the effect of charges and creating systems to limit their effect, you can create financial well-being all the more effectively and protect a greater amount of your well-deserved cash over the long haul.

7. Oversee Obligation and Construct Your Credit

As you create financial well-being, you'll begin to find it advantageous to assume the obligation to subsidize different purchases or speculations. You might pay for things with a Mastercard to procure focuses or compensates. You could apply for a home loan for a home or second home, a home value credit for home upgrades, or a vehicle credit to buy a vehicle. Perhaps you'll need to take out individual credit to assist with beginning a business or put resources into another person's.

Be that as it may, it's critical to deal with your debt cautiously, assuming an excess of obligations could obstruct your advancement toward your substantial financial foundation objectives. To oversee obligations, be aware of your outstanding debt compared to revenue proportions and ensure that your obligation installments are reasonable and acceptable for you. You ought to likewise plan to take care of exorbitant interest debt, for example, Visa obligations, as fast as conceivable to try not to pay extreme interest charges. Be careful about a factor or customizable loan cost items or those with expanded installments, as changes to the economy or your own conditions can rapidly make those obligations unmanageable.

Without a doubt, in the event that you fall into debt, your FICO rating can be affected in a bad way, and assuming you default on your obligations, you could face individual liquidation.

Keeping a Decent FICO Rating

Constructing and keeping a decent FICO rating is a significant part of developing and protecting your abundance over the long haul. You'll partake in lower financing costs and better terms on your advances in the event that you have serious areas of strength for a set of experiences and a high FICO rating, which can save you many dollars in revenue charges over the long run.

The following are a couple of key advances that you can take to keep a decent FICO rating:

Take care of your bills on time.
Perhaps the main element that influences your FICO rating is your installment history. To keep a decent FICO rating, you ought to try to cover your bills on time, like clockwork. Late installments, regardless of whether they're a couple of days late, can adversely affect your FICO rating.

Keep your credit usage low.
Your credit usage, or how much credit you're utilizing compared with the amount you have available, is another significant element that influences your FICO assessment. To keep a decent FICO rating, you ought to keep your

credit usage below 28% of your accessible credit.

Screen your credit report

It's smart to check your credit report routinely to ensure that all the data is exact and forward-thinking. Today, there are a few administrations that will give you a credit report for nothing. Mistakes in your credit report can adversely affect your financial assessment, so it's critical to question any errors you find.

Try not to open such a large number of new records.

Each time you apply for credit, it can adversely affect your financial assessment. To keep a decent FICO rating, you ought to try not to open an excessive number of new records in a brief timeframe. Note, in any case, that on the off chance that you don't use Mastercards or need more credit lines open, you might succumb to not having an adequate record as a consumer.

Thus, open some Mastercards and take out certain advances; however, don't go overboard.

By following these means and pursuing great credit routines, you can keep a decent FICO rating and expand your control over the long haul.

Would it be a good idea for me to invest or take care of my debt?

In the event that you have exorbitant premium obligations, for example, many Mastercard charges, it ordinarily seems OK to take care of them before you contribute. Hardly any speculations at any point pay however much Visa charges. Whenever you've taken care of your obligations, divert that additional cash to reserve funds and ventures. Furthermore, attempt to cover your Visa balance every month, whenever the situation allows, to try not to owe interest from here on out.

How much cash do I have to purchase a common mortgage?

Common asset organizations have different least-introductory speculation prerequisites to get everything rolling, frequently starting at about $600. From that point on, you can ordinarily contribute less. A few shared assets will defer their underlying essentials in the event that you focus on effective financial planning with a standard total every month. You can likewise purchase common assets and trade-exchanged reserve shares through a business firm, some of which don't charge anything for opening a record.

Trade-exchange reserves?

Trade-exchange reserves are speculation pools similar to shared reserves. A key distinction is that their portions are exchanged on stock trades (instead of traded through a specific asset organization). In some cases, they also charge lower expenses. You can likewise get them, along with stocks and bonds, through a business firm.

The primary concern

While pyramid schemes now and again might be tempting, the dependable method for creating financial momentum is through ordinary saving, effective money management, and persistently permitting that cash to develop after some time. Beginning small is fine. The significant thing is to begin, and an ambitious beginning-bring in cash and, afterward, save and contribute it astutely. Safeguard your resources with protection, and limit your duty openness.

Keep in mind that creating financial well-being is an excursion, not an objective. Commend your victories en route, and don't get deterred by misfortunes or impediments. With persistence, discipline, and a reasonable vision of your objectives, you can make monetary progress and create financial momentum over the long haul.

CHAPTER 4: Boosting Your Income

While reasonable planning and monetary discipline can assist you with capitalizing on the assets you have, there are cutoff points to the amount you can scale back. Then again, the possibility of building your pay is practically boundless. This carries us to Section 4: Helping Your Pay, a significant stage on your roadmap to monetary strengthening.

In this section, we will investigate various methodologies and roads to upgrade your acquiring potential. Whether you are hoping to expand your current pay, leave for another vocation, or transform your interests and gifts into extra income streams, this section is your far-reaching manual for accomplishing only that.

Why Helping Your Pay Matters

Prior to diving into the how-tos of pay improvement, we should initially comprehend the reason why it's a vital component of monetary prosperity. A higher salary provides you with the necessary resources to productively accomplish your monetary objectives. It can facilitate your obligation reimbursement, speed up your reserve funds for significant life achievements like purchasing a home or sending your youngsters to school, and speed up your excursion to independence from the rat race and security.

In addition, helping your pay can likewise upgrade your general personal satisfaction. It can bear the cost of giving you the chance to appreciate more encounters, seek after your interests, and ease monetary pressure. Monetary steadiness, all things considered, isn't just about having sufficient cash to cover your essential necessities; it's tied in with having the opportunity to carry on with life according to your own preferences.

The Significance of Helping Your Pay

Helping your pay is something other than a monetary desire; it's a critical driver of monetary prosperity. Here's the reason it is important:

Quicker Objective Accomplishment: A higher pay speeds up your advancement towards monetary achievements, whether it's taking care of obligations, purchasing a home, or building retirement savings.

Working on Personal Satisfaction: Extra pay can upgrade your general personal satisfaction, offering you the opportunity to appreciate encounters, seek after interests, and lessen monetary pressure.

Adaptability and Decisions: Expanded pay gives you more decisions and adaptability in the way you carry on with your life. You can pursue choices in light of your inclinations, not simply monetary requirements.

Resilience: A higher salary can assist you with enduring monetary tempests, like unforeseen costs or financial slumps, without sweat.

Surveying Your Ongoing Income

Before you can help your pay, having an unmistakable image of your ongoing monetary situation is fundamental. This includes considering your current types of revenue, like your compensation, and any extra income streams, like rental pay or profits from ventures. Recording your ongoing revenue streams will act as a gauge against which you can quantify your advancement.

Whenever you've surveyed your ongoing pay, now is the right time to lay out reasonable pay objectives. What monetary goals would you say you are endeavoring to accomplish? Is it true or not that you are hoping to take care of obligations, save for a getaway, or fabricate a powerful retirement store? Laying out clear and achievable pay objectives will give you the inspiration and direction expected to successfully help your income.

Investigating Pay-Supporting Techniques

In view of your objectives, now is the right time to investigate the huge number of pay-supporting techniques accessible to you. This part will dive into a few roads for expanding your pay, including:

1. **Professional success:** improving your abilities, looking for advancements, or investigating more lucrative open positions inside your ongoing field.

2. **Part-time jobs:** Seeking part-time gigs or independent work that line up with your abilities and interests.

3. **Entrepreneurship:** wandering into the universe of business proprietorship,

whether it's a little startup, an internet-based store, or a counseling administration

4. Venture Pay: creating extra pay through ventures, like profits from stocks, interest from bonds, or rental pay from land.

5. **Automated revenue:** making computerized revenue sources similar to those from licensed innovation, offshoot advertising, or pay-creating sites

6. **Adapting leisure activities:** Transforming your interests and leisure activities into pay-producing exercises, like selling fine art or specialties, offering music illustrations, or contributing to a blog about your inclinations.

7. **Instruction and Expertise Improvement:** Getting new abilities or affirmations that can open doors to more lucrative professions is amazing.

Every one of these systems offers remarkable benefits and might be more suitable for various people and conditions. Whether you're keen on differentiating your pay sources, chasing after your enterprising dreams, or basically augmenting your acquiring expectations in your present place of employment, you'll track down reasonable exhortations and significant stages in this part to assist you with the beginning.

Beating difficulties and hindrances

While the possibility of helping your pay is without a doubt energizing, it's not without its difficulties. Adjusting numerous revenue sources, overseeing time successfully, and exploring potential mishaps are all important for the excursion. In this part, we will likewise address normal hindrances and give techniques for conquering them.

Moreover, we'll underline the significance of keeping a solid balance between serious and fun activities and staying balanced. Chasing after expanded pay ought to upgrade your general personal satisfaction, not bring it down.

The Master Plan: Adjusting Pay to Monetary Objectives

Eventually, the objective of helping your pay is to adjust it to your more extensive monetary goals. Whether you expect to accomplish monetary freedom, resign early, or give a superior future to your family, your expanded pay ought to be an integral asset in understanding those fantasies.

All through this section, we'll accentuate the meaning of compelling monetary preparation. Your financial endeavors ought to consistently incorporate your planning, reserve funds, and speculation techniques to make an extensive monetary arrangement that pushes you toward your objectives.

4.1 Optimizing Your Earning

Is it true that you are prepared to unlock your potential? Whether you're searching for some additional money as an afterthought or want to transform your energy into a full-time gig, boosting your revenue stream is vital. In any case, with so many choices out there, it tends to be difficult to tell where to begin. That is the reason we've assembled this extensive manual to assist you with exploring the universe of revenue sources and finding the recipe for progress. From acquisition to automated revenue, we'll cover all that you really want to be aware of to open up your procuring potential and achieve independence from the rat race. So sit back, unwind, and prepare to assume command over your monetary future!

The Various Kinds of Revenue Sources

There is a wide range of kinds of revenue streams out there, and everyone enjoys their own benefits and detriments. One of the most widely recognized is procured pay, which is cash you procure through working on a task or offering support. This can be anything from full-time compensation to independent work as an afterthought.

One more kind of revenue stream is automated revenue, which permits you to bring in cash without effectively working for it. This could incorporate things like investment properties, interests in stocks or land, or, in any event, selling computerized items on the web.

Then there's portfolio pay, which comes from speculations like stocks and bonds. There's a capital increase in pay, which you procure by selling a resource for more than you paid for it.

Each kind of revenue stream has its own novel advantages and dangers, depending on your singular objectives and conditions. By understanding these various choices and investigating what turns out best for you and, you'll be well on your way to unlocking your potential and achieving independence from the rat race.

Instructions to Augment Your Potential Revenue Source

To amplify your potential revenue source, the initial step is to distinguish all potential types of revenue. This incorporates your essential occupation as well as any second jobs or independent work you can do. Consider utilizing sites like Fiverr or Upwork to track down extra work.

Then, assess your abilities and check whether there are ways you can adapt them. For instance, in the event that you have the ability to compose, think about beginning a blog or independent composition as an afterthought.

One more method for amplifying your profit is by putting resources into yourself through schooling and preparing programs. Take courses that will improve your range of abilities and make you more significant in the gig market.

As well as expanding your revenue sources, it's vital to successfully oversee them. Make a spending plan that considers reserve funds and puts resources into long-term monetary plans, for example, retirement records or property ventures.

Recall that amplifying your potential revenue stream requires persistence and devotion. Continue to push forward towards new open doors while making a point to keep up with balance in all everyday issues, including well-being, connections, and self-awareness.

The Advantages of Boosting Your Potential Revenue Source

Boosting your potential revenue stream has a few advantages that can further develop your monetary prosperity. Having various sources of income implies you are not totally subject to one source of income. This gives a security net in the event that one source evaporates or encounters a slump.

Boosting your purchasing potential likewise permits you to accomplish monetary objectives quickly. In the event that you have more cash coming in, you can save more and contribute more towards accomplishing your drawn-out monetary targets.

Expanding your revenue streams can prompt more prominent work fulfillment and individual satisfaction. Seeking after extra types of revenue beyond your essential profession means considering investigating new interests and interests that may not be imaginable within the limits of conventional work.

Moreover, expanding your profit through different channels empowers you to create financial momentum after some time by producing recurring, automated revenue through ventures like stocks or land.

Augmenting your potential revenue stream is indispensable for accomplishing independence from the rat race and adaptability while opening ways to investigate new roads for development both monetarily and actually.

The Dangers of Not Augmenting Your Potential Revenue Source

Not expanding your potential revenue stream is a significant gamble that many individuals ignore. By restricting yourself to only one kind of revenue, you are putting yourself helpless before financial variances or changes inside your industry.

All depending entirely on a task, compensation can be dangerous as it may not generally be sufficient to cover life's costs. It likewise implies that any surprising costs will probably emerge from investment funds, as opposed to from an extra type of revenue.

One more gamble is stagnation in vocation development and improvement. Without investigating other expected kinds of revenue, it might become challenging for people to acquire new abilities or expand their expert organization and experience.

Moreover, not having various floods of pay puts people in a tough spot during seasons of emergency like a financial downturn or worldwide pandemic. A different scope of income channels gives more monetary soundness during capricious occasions.

Neglecting to boost your potential revenue stream could mean botched open doors for individual and expert development while additionally leaving you powerless financially.
The most effective method to get everything rolling is to expand your potential revenue source.
Since it has become so undeniably obvious about the various kinds of revenue sources and how to augment your possible profit, now is the right time to begin. Here are some pointers on how to get started effectively:

1. Distinguish your abilities: Begin by recognizing your abilities and interests. What do you appreciate doing? What are you great at? This will assist you with figuring out what kind of revenue stream is most appropriate for you.

2. Research open doors: Properly investigate things and investigate the different open doors accessible in your chosen field. Search for online stages or sites that proposition independent business related to obtainment or whatever other class where there is popularity.

3. Foster an Arrangement: Whenever you've distinguished an open door that lines up with your abilities, foster an arrangement on the best way to adapt it, involving equations for money estimation.

4. Make a move: Now is the ideal time to make a move! Buckle down, keep on

track, and be predictable in conveying quality outcomes for clients.

5. Assess Results Consistently: Routinely assess your headway with the goal that you can make essential changes en route if necessary.

By following these means, anybody can begin expanding their potential revenue stream, no matter what their ability level or experience level!

In this day and age, there are various chances to amplify your potential revenue source. From the customary 8-4 or 9-5 occupation to beginning a part-time job or putting resources into stocks, the potential outcomes are unfathomable. By expanding your revenue sources and tracking down ways of expanding every one, you can unlock your full procurement potential.

It's important to remember that expanding your revenue stream takes time, exertion, and devotion. Be that as it may, the advantages of doing so can change lives. Besides the fact that it provides monetary security and solidity, you should additionally consider more opportunity and adaptability in the way you carry on with your life.

Standby no longer to begin augmenting your potential revenue source. Whether it's by acquiring new abilities or investigating various open doors, make a move today toward opening your full potential!

4.2. Explore Additional Streams of Income

In the present dynamic and steadily developing economy, depending exclusively on a single kind of revenue can restrict your monetary development and security. By broadening your revenue sources, you can make various roads for income age, prompting more noteworthy monetary steadiness and the potential for huge pay. Here are strong methodologies that can assist you with creating different surges of critical pay and opening new doors for monetary achievement. Present the idea of creating numerous surges of pay and feature the advantages of doing so. Stress the significance of having assorted pay sources to moderate dangers and accomplish monetary objectives.

It may very well be trying to think of automated revenue thoughts; however, on the off chance that you're hoping to get more cash flow without adding a lot of work to your plate, it tends to be a rewarding experience. Recurring, automated revenue is tied in with expanding your income latently.

Certain individuals even allude to it as "bringing in cash for your rest." That is the very thing that makes acquiring recurring, automated revenue so appealing. There might be some forthright work; however, after that is finished, you'll acquire repeating pay latently. In this way, to amplify your procuring potential, you can add various automated sources of income to help your income.

What is automated revenue?

Automated revenue is the point at which you bring in cash without expecting to chip away at an hourly reason for it. Contrasted with dynamic pay, like working an everyday job or outsourcing, automated revenue sometimes requires forthright work to get everything rolling, except in the end, cash procured is made during the entire day, including while you rest.

Finding recurring, automated revenue thoughts can permit you to increase your profit without matching your work hours continuously to accomplish that pay.

Repeating mechanized income can be an unbelievable strategy for helping you deliver extra pay, whether you're running a seasonal job or basically endeavoring to get some extra combination consistently, especially as extension fumes generally through the economy. Mechanized income can help you earn earnestly during extraordinary times and tide you over expecting you to suddenly become jobless. If you tenaciously eliminate time from work, then again accepting that development will sever your purchasing power.

With computerized income, you can have cash coming in even as you seek after your fundamental work. Then again, if you're prepared to foster areas of strength for repeating, mechanized income, you ought to kick back a little. For sure, a computerized income gives you extra security.

Furthermore, expecting that you're worried about having the choice to save enough of your benefit to meet your retirement goals, making monetary energy through repeating, mechanized income is a method that could connect with you, too.

Mechanized income isn't...

Your work. Overall, repeating, mechanized income isn't paid that comes from something you've been substantially drawn in with, for instance, the wages you obtain from an errand.

Some 10 go-to-get Passive Income Ideas.

1. Market digital items

Recurring, automated revenue thoughts can likewise be basically as straightforward as selling advanced items. For instance, you can make a web-based course, sell calculation sheets, make music, logo plans, or some other sort of computerized item. Some Etsy vendors sell printables, an exceptionally famous sort of computerized item. The advantage of selling advanced items is that the possible cost is your time, assuming you make them yourself. Everybody has the right stuff to essentially make one explicit sort of computerized item. You'll have to showcase your items, except if you're selling in a commercial center for that kind of computerized item. Notwithstanding, you can procure pay from every deal or month to month through a membership administration. Whether you're planning a web-based course or planning printables for instructors, there's a method for bringing in cash for web-based sales of computerized items.

2. Begin a YouTube channel.

Not at all like most online entertainment applications, YouTube is one of the main informal communities that permit you to procure promotion income as a substance maker. While some powerhouses post on YouTube about their lives or make viral content to create the most potential perspectives, you can likewise procure recurring, automated revenue from YouTube as an entrepreneur. For instance, in the event that you own an outsourcing site with different moving items, you could make an item survey YouTube channel so individuals can see the items in real life. Then, at that point, you'll procure recurring, automated revenue from your business and your YouTube channel, which likewise assists with showcasing your business. To procure automated revenue from the very beginning, you can make YouTube shorts. If not, you'll require somewhere around 1,000 endorsers and 4,000 public watch hours to make this your automated source of income.

3. Get interested by lending cash.

Incalculable distributed loaning programs permit you to bring in revenue by loaning cash to individuals. You can acquire recurring, automated revenue with very little capital. Beneficially, you get your cash back, and you acquire extra pay. It's practically similar to having an exorbitant premium investment account. The advantage to doing this is that you're helping somebody out of luck. There might be organizations that can't stand to purchase new gear that will help them drastically. In this way, it very well may be a net decent thing you do to help individuals while likewise procuring recurring, automated revenue for sure.

4. Dividend Stock Investment

Putting resources into stocks is one of the most well-known automated revenue ideas since it just requires some exploration. In the event that you're hoping to add a recurring source of income that helps you pay somewhat more, consider putting resources into profit stocks. Contingent upon the organization, you'll procure profits routinely, like each quarter. Something to note is that a few house and vehicle insurance agencies are likewise on the financial exchange. At times, you can pick an insurance agency that will deliver you profits for being their client. It could be paid every year, except that it actually assists you with acquiring latent knowledge without expecting to accomplish any forthright work other than joining. Concerning profit stocks, you'll have to explore the best organizations that deliver profits consistently to pick the best ones. Besides, when your stock has value, you can sell it for a benefit.

5. Begin blogging

A blog is a resource that permits you to procure recurring, automated revenue; however, you'll have to do a lot of hard work to get things moving. You'll have to make different search engine-oriented blog entries in a particular specialty. To begin the blog, you'll need to begin with the most popular catchphrases first. Then, at that point, as those articles rank, you'll expand your catchphrase decisions two or three degrees more extensively. And afterward, you'll rehash that as you've begun positioning for different watchwords in your specialty. There are different kinds of automated sources of income you can acquire from publishing content on a blog. For instance, you can bring in cash from elite bargains, partner promotion, supported posts, publicizing, selling physical or computerized items, or, in any event, selling your administrations. There are so many recurring sources of income that come from contributing to a blog that it merits a portion of the difficult work involved in making it a triumph.

6. App creation

The absolute most well-known organizations are applications. From TikTok to FitBit, there's a requirement for a new application in countless various specialties. For instance, you can begin an application in wellbeing, virtual entertainment, picture altering, home security, secret word on the board, and so on. You don't have to create the application yourself, by the same token.

Assuming that you have some capital, you can enlist designers to assemble the application you need for your vision. To prevail in the application space, most application proprietors have numerous applications in various specialties to work out their recurring sources of income. You'll require an income to deal with the application updates, showcasing, and independent expenses.

Nonetheless, having an application can assist with producing recurring, automated revenue that scales without any problem. An automated revenue methodology for application creation is to work for iOS, Android, and, in addition, a web rendition. By having a web rendition of your application, you diminish the risk of getting your application restricted from an application store with the goal that you can hold your clients. You might in fact fabricate a Shopify application in the event that you're in the online business space.

7. Print-on-request business

Like outsourcing, print-on-request organizations are another recurring, automated revenue source you can attempt. With print-on-request, you'll have to make plans for dress or purchase proficient plans from a site like Innovative Market, 99 Plans, or other expert visual computerization asset destinations. You'll have to visit the Shopify Application Store to find print-on-request applications that will fabricate your plans, bundle them, and ship them to your clients. You'll likewise have to do a large number of the commonplace sign-up advances, for example, pursuing Shopify, BigCommerce, or some other popular online business web designer. At last, you'll have to modify your site, pick the best specialty, and oversee promotion and client care.

8. Real estate investment

One of the most amazing automated revenue ideas that has assisted numerous people with acquiring recurring, automated revenue is putting resources into land. The best chance to purchase generally changes depending on the city or country. In any case, as individuals moved towards remote work during the pandemic, more individuals have been purchasing more properties. That implies townhouses are the open door, essentially at the hour of composition. You can acquire rental payments by leasing the property or posting it on Airbnb. The main disadvantage of putting resources into land is that there's forthright speculation included. You'll have to put down an initial investment of 20% in the event that this isn't your most memorable property. You'll likewise have to have a positive FICO rating. Land financial planning isn't indicating that things are pulling back. What to acknowledge is that there's a limited amount of land on the planet, making possessing it significant after some time. That is the reason real estate market declines are uncommon in certain nations

9. You can also affiliate.

Any person with a resource can turn into a partner and procure recurring, automated revenue. A partner can advance different organizations by means of their email list, online course, blog, application, site, web-based entertainment, or even visitor posting. At last, possessing a resource with a major crowd has the effect of turning into a member. In any case, obviously, everybody begins with nothing. So you can fabricate a resource with partner interfaces almost immediately. It'll simply take more time to procure your partner bonuses.

Furthermore, contingent upon the partner programme, you probably won't have the option to pull out until you hit a particular dollar sum. In any case, being a partner can be a worthwhile business. One of the most famous subsidiary projects is the Sprocket partner program, which permits you to procure commissions for each client you allude to in Sprocket.

10. Investment in profitable businesses

As recently referenced, putting resources into stocks is a recurring, automated revenue activity you can do to put resources into organizations.

Be that as it may, putting resources into organizations should likewise be possible before the organization's initial public offering. Being a financial backer doesn't require a large number of dollars to get everything rolling. You can turn into a private supporter, which requires a normal venture of between $25,000 and $100,000 to a business that you'll procure value from. Then, when the organization sells, you'll procure the level of the deal, contingent upon what you arranged. For instance, financial backers can arrange the level of the business and the variety of their ventures. Thus, on the off chance that you're hoping to produce recurring, automated revenue, this doesn't need forthright work. Notwithstanding, a few financial backers decide to tutor the organizations to guarantee that they get their cash back, to say the least.

CHAPTER 5: Financial Freedom Plan

Accomplishing independence from the rat race is an objective that many desire, and for good reason. Independence from the rat race addresses a daily existence where you have the assets and independence to pursue decisions that line up with your qualities, interests, and long-term targets. It's a condition of monetary prosperity where cash works for you as opposed to the other way around.

Independence from the rat race is a critical piece of any fruitful life. As a matter of fact, without it, you might wind up battling to carry on with the existence you need. Whether you mean to resign early, venture to the far corners of the planet, or simply have more monetary adaptability, understanding and executing the four keys to independence from the rat race can assist you with arriving at your objectives. Here, we'll investigate every one of the keys and give tips on the best way to accomplish them. We'll likewise talk about a portion of the normal entanglements that could keep you from arriving at your monetary objectives and give some counsel on the most proficient method to keep away from them. By following these tips, you'll be on your way to gaining effective independence from the rat race organizer. So prepare to open your future with the four keys to independence from the rat race!

- **Freedom for Financial Independence: The Principal Objective**

The primary objective of independence from the rat race is to give you a guide to a superior future. By getting some margin to outline your objectives and recognizing the means you really want to take to accomplish them, you'll be one bit closer to accomplishing your fantasies.

One of the main parts of independence from the rat race is making a practical timetable. Setting courses of events assists you with remaining focused, and try not to postpone significant assignments until some other time. It's additionally critical to be adaptable with your timetable; don't allow unbending assumptions to impede accomplishing your objectives.

The next key component of independence from the rat race is to make a spending plan. Making a financial plan permits you to follow your spending and see where you can adapt. By understanding where your cash is going, you'll have the option to arrive at better conclusions about where to apportion your assets.

The last key component of independence from the rat race is to make a reserve fund plan. A reserve fund plan is fundamental to having sufficient cash to cover unexpected costs. Having an investment fund plan will likewise permit you to arrive at your monetary objectives quickly.

By following these four keys to independence from the rat race, you'll be en route to a superior future.

- **Freedom for Financial Independence: What You'll Need**

If you have any desire to accomplish independence from the rat race in 2023, you'll have to do some preparation. Furthermore, arranging begins with understanding what you'll need to accomplish your objectives.

To have a fruitful monetary future in 2023, you'll have to have a strong comprehension of your funds and your ways of managing money. You'll likewise have to have an arrangement for effective money management and saving.

The following are the four vital keys to opening your future right now:

1. Have an arrangement for your pay. You'll have to have an arrangement for distributing your pay towards the various regions of your monetary future. This incorporates your drawn-out investment funds, your transient costs, and your retirement investment funds.

2. Have an arrangement for your spending. You'll have to have an arrangement for designating your spending towards the various regions of your monetary future. This incorporates your drawn-out reserve funds, your transient costs, and your retirement investment funds.

3. Have an arrangement for your ventures. You'll have to have an arrangement for designating your speculations towards the various regions of your monetary future. This incorporates your drawn-out reserve

funds, your momentary costs, and your retirement reserve funds.

4. Have an arrangement for your life. You'll have to have an arrangement for disbursing your significant investment towards the various regions of your monetary future. This incorporates your drawn-out reserve funds, your momentary costs, and your retirement reserve funds.

By following these four key keys, you'll be en route to achieving independence from the rat race in 2023 and beyond.

- **Freedom for Financial Independence: How to Arrive**

There are four key things that you want to zero in on to achieve independence from the rat race in 2023. These are: saving, effective money management, arriving at your objectives, and living below your means.

Saving is the main step in light of the fact that without a pad of reserve funds, you cannot stand to fall into obligations or face any surprising costs. You ought to plan to save no less than 30% of your pay every month, which will permit you to take care of unforeseen expenses or crises.

Putting is one more key to achieving independence from the rat race. You ought to plan to have something like 3 to a half years of everyday costs saved if there should be an occurrence of an unforeseen cost or an employment cutback. This will permit you to weather any monetary storm and keep your head above water.

You will likewise have to arrive at your objectives to achieve independence from the rat race. At the point when you have explicit focus at the top of the priority list, it will be simpler to pursue them and remain propelled. Laying out short- and long-term objectives will assist you with staying on track and on target.

In conclusion, it means quite a bit to live below your means. You ought to attempt to live within your means and try not to assume pointless obligations. This will assist you with setting aside cash and arriving at your monetary objectives all the more without any problem.

By following these four key tips, you will be en route to independence from the rat race.

- **Freedom for Financial Independence: The Four Keys to Opening Your Future**

The year 2023 is rapidly drawing nearer, and many individuals are still making progress toward their independence from the rat race objectives. The Four Keys to Opening Your Future are vital to comprehend if you have any desire to accomplish your monetary objectives in the year 2023.

The Four Keys to Opening Your Future are:

Be Instructed

You must be instructed about the various choices and methodologies that are accessible to you. You must learn about the duty regulations that will influence you and comprehend the different venture vehicles that are accessible to you. You should be proactive and understand what to do assuming you are confronted with an extraordinary occasion or, on the other hand, on the off chance that the market takes a slump.

Have an arrangement

You want to have an arrangement. You want to understand what your drawn-out objectives are and the way in which you will accomplish them. You should be focused and adhere to your arrangement. You should be reasonable in your assumptions and understand what you can and can't accomplish.

Have the right assets.

You really want the right assets to assist you with accomplishing your objectives. You want the monetary assets to put resources in the right places and the duty assets to take advantage of your profit. You really want a significant investment to invest important energy.

Make a move.

You need to make a move to accomplish your independence from the rat race objectives. You need to begin today and roll out little improvements that will prompt greater changes from now on. You need to remain on track and continue to push ahead.

Freedom for Financial Independence: The Main Concern

2023 is rapidly drawing nearer to its end, and many individuals are considering how they ought to plan for their future. While nobody replies to this inquiry, there are four key rules that will assist you in opening your future.

Guideline 1: Assume responsibility for your cash

If you have any desire to achieve independence from the rat race in 2023, you really want to assume responsibility for your cash. This implies making a financial plan, adhering to it, and putting resources into yourself and your future.

Guideline 2: Make an Arrangement

Making an arrangement is critical to progress. Without an arrangement, you will be hit with confusion and vulnerability. An arrangement will frame your short--, mid-, and long-haul objectives and give you methodologies to accomplish them.

Guideline 3: Remain Inspired

Remaining inspired is vital to progress. You might end up confronting difficulties, yet assuming you remain fixed on your objectives, you will ultimately contact them.

Guideline 4: Remain Adaptable

The world is continually changing, and that implies your arrangements might have to change too. Be ready to make changes, and feel free to explore. In the event that you do this accurately, you will actually want to arrive at your independence from the rat race objectives in 2023 and beyond.

5.1. Setting Reasonable Financial Goals

Do you feel like you're making a good attempt to make the ideal choices with your money, but you can never appear to excel? Or, on the other hand, have you been working extremely hard, yet you don't have a lot to show for it towards the month's end?

Definitely, things like expansion and downturn are genuine and can feel like immense snags. Be that as it may, in the event that you set no objectives for your cash, you'll presumably still feel like you're wasting your time—in any event when the economy isn't insane.

To at long last make progress with your cash, you really want to define a few monetary objectives. Relax; it's not as convoluted as it sounds. I'll walk you through how to lay out monetary objectives bit by bit.

What Is a Monetary Objective?

A monetary objective is any arrangement you have for your cash. You can have momentary monetary objectives (like setting aside $1,000) or long-haul monetary objectives (like money management for retirement). You ought to lay out objectives for each aspect of your life; however, having explicit monetary objectives assists you with, in a real sense, putting your cash where your objective is.

Also, I can't discuss monetary objectives without discussing the Child Steps. Attempting to conclude how to manage your cash can feel as overpowering as picking what to watch on Netflix. There are countless choices, and everybody has an assessment.

Would it be advisable for you to take care of your obligations? Save for your children's school. Purchase a house. Contribute to retirement? The 7 Gradual Steps slice through all the disarray and give you a way to do everything! It assists you with zeroing in on each objective in turn, so you can make more advancements with your cash and experience monetary harmony.

Thus, on the off chance that you do not know what monetary objective to pursue first, begin by taking this fast evaluation to figure out what gradual step you're on.

Five Smart Moves Towards Laying Out Monetary Objectives

1. *Make your objective explicit.*

One explanation for individuals' neglect to meet their objectives is the grounds that they put forth objectives that are excessively unclear. You could say, "I need to be better with cash." In any case, how might that really affect you? Tighten it down!

Imagine a scenario where you choose to handle your obligation. That is a particular region of your cash to zero in on. Presently, we should discuss how to separate this objective much more.

2. *Make your objective quantifiable.*

Alright, so you need to take care of your obligations. Presently, it is the right time to pick a careful sum—something you can gauge to be aware of on the off chance that you hit your objective or not.

While being totally debt-free ought to be your definitive objective (that is, Gradual Step 2), it's really smart to separate that objective into more modest pieces. Like that, you won't feel excessively crushed before you even begin.

In this way, perhaps you have $60,000 of all-out debt, yet you need to begin by paying off a $20,000 understudy loan first. Hello, that is a quantifiable objective.

3. Give yourself a cutoff time.

Here's how things are: It's really enticing to hesitate on your objectives on the off chance that they aren't time-delicate. According to creator Benny Lewis, "There are seven days in seven days, and sometime in the not so distant future' isn't one of them." Quit saying sometime in the future. You really want to give yourself a cutoff time and make it sensible, yet in addition, it is somewhat testing.

Back to the understudy loan model: When would you like to hit your objective? To pay off

$20,000 in one year, that implies you'll have to pay about $1,670 every month. Is this conceivable yet, in addition to being somewhat of a stretch? Assuming this is the case, great!

4. Ensure they're your own objectives.

We should discuss comparisons briefly. It's not difficult to glance around at what others are doing and feel like you ought to make it happen as well. Are your neighbors driving the most recent model vehicles? Is that one young lady on Instagram continuously taking lavish getaways? Hello, congratulations! In any case, that doesn't mean you really want to do likewise.

At the point when we contrast ourselves with others, we're playing a game we won't ever win. In this way, ensure you're laying out monetary objectives that check out for you. As such, the fact that every one of your companions is requiring second home loans for redesigned kitchens doesn't mean you ought to. Put the blinders on, center around your path, and cross your own end goal. What's more, be sure about why you've picked the objectives you have.

5. Get your objective on paper.

Did you know you're bound to accomplish your objectives, assuming that you record them on paper? That's right, it's valid—something doesn't add up about putting pen to paper that assists you with focusing on the main job.

In this way, feel free to explicitly state your objectives. Then, at that point, stick them in your vehicle, in your work area, or on your bathroom mirror. Type them in the Notes application on your telephone, take a screen capture, and set it as your backdrop so it's the principal thing you see when you get your telephone. Keeping your objectives where you can see them will keep you on target and motivated.

Five Normal Monetary Objectives

With such a lot of cash "guidance" drifting around, it tends to be difficult to tell which monetary objectives are ideal for you. Like I said previously, begin with the child moving towards sorting out their higher-perspective cash objectives. In any case, there are likewise more modest objectives that can assist you with hitting those achievements.

Here are probably the most well-known monetary objectives individuals set and tips on the best way to get them going:

1. *Make and adhere to a spending plan.*

Not exclusively is planning one of the top monetary objectives individuals set each new year, but at the same time, it's the establishment you ought to construct all your other cash objectives.

A spending plan is the means by which you make progress with your cash. It's an arrangement for what's coming in (your pay) and what's going out (your costs). You're letting your cash know where to go, rather than pondering where it went. So you can feel sure you're moving towards your objective consistently.

Planning assists you with picking up speed in each space of your funds. In the event that you're now planning, bravo! In the event that not, begin free of charge with EveryDollar.

2. *Develop a rainy-day account.*

Life occurs. However, you can be ready for any cash issues that come your way, assuming you have sufficient cash set aside. I'm talking about vehicle inconvenience, clinical costs, and busted latrines (you know, a portion of the most terrible pieces of being a grown-up). Yet, when you have a rainy day account, you can rest well around evening time, realizing you will not need to venture into the red to cover those minutes.

Begin with the monetary objective of having $1,000 in reserve funds. Then, assuming you have an obligation, now is the ideal time to take that out. (I'll discuss that in a moment.) From that point onward, you need to develop a completely subsidized backup stash with 3-6 months of costs. (Once more, this is completely shrouded in the Child Steps—the demonstrated arrangement to assist you with assuming command over your cash.)

At the point when you have a just-in-case account, you're prepared for those "life occurs" minutes. Rather than being stressed over what could occur straight away, you'll feel sure that you have cash saved to manage it.

3. *Escape obligation.*

Assuming that you have obligations, now is the right time to quit fooling around with taking care of them. Every last bit of it. Definitely, I realize that might appear to be unimaginable at this moment, particularly assuming you have a few major numbers looking straight at you. In any case, being underwater doesn't push you ahead;

it keeps you down. You can't excel with your cash assuming that it's continuously going to installments.

4. *Put something aside for your retirement dreams.*

Pause for a minute to envision your optimal retirement. Would you like to get together with the grandchildren and make a beeline for Disney each Christmas? Visit another state with your partner once a quarter. Peruse each book on your racks. Take up a great side interest.

Regardless of what you're longing for in the future, you'll need great retirement speculation now to make it a reality. In this way, when you're without obligation and have that completely supported backup stash, I believe you should begin money management by paying 15% of your family for retirement. Furthermore, prepare to be blown away. At the point when you have zero obligation, all that cash you were shipping off installments is presently speculation fuel for your retirement dreams!

5. *Spend less and save more.*

Lots of individuals toss out the objective of "I need to spend less" or "I need to save more" without contemplating what it means to do those things in fact. In any case, you must be deliberate about your cash propensities.

Make and adhere to your spending plan consistently; find bargains, use coupons, and pay cash. What's more, here's a major one: Figure out how to say no—even to yourself! I'm not saying you ought to never have a great time. Yet, to set aside cash, it will take some preparation and a life-changing approach.

Lastly, here's one of my number one methods for spending less and saving more: Plan your feasts! Food is where most Americans overspend, and feast arranging is the manner in which you get control over that. Look at my free week-after-week dinner organizer and Staple Reserve funds manual to learn how to get a good deal on food.

An Illustration of a Monetary Objective in Real Life

Alright, so now that I've gone over the essentials of monetary objective preparation, let me provide you with an illustration of how this can function in actuality.

Some time back, my better half, McCarthy, and I chose to fabricate a house. Before that, any additional pay we acquired went directly to our overall investment funds. However, I knew building a house would cost a tonne, and arbitrary costs would undoubtedly spring up during the cycle.

Thus, we made it an objective to set aside however much we could—explicitly towards our home. Keeping in mind that setting aside that much cash appeared to be exceptionally difficult, separating it into month-to-month objectives gave us a lot of force. Having an arrangement for our cash made our fantasy conceivable; however, it likewise made the interaction fun!

It likewise kept my burning through propensities (otherwise known as dependencies—trust me, it's a thing) under control. Realizing my cash was going towards something that I truly believed persuaded me to spend less What's more, despite the fact that there were minutes when we felt exhausted—I mean, there were a few days when all I needed to do was unwind and burn through cash—tracking down imaginative ways of hitting our objective quicker kept us on target every month.

Past that, it was character-building. During a period of our marriage, we'll continuously have the option to reflect and realize we achieved something hard together. It developed an association among us and happiness in my own heart. Presently, I understand that the advantages of the cycle are worth more than the new house.

Why is putting forth monetary objectives significant?

Having an objective assists you with being more future-disapproved with your cash. You'll begin to perceive how each choice you make adds up and matters to your by and large monetary well-being.

For instance, in the event that you don't have monetary objectives, it's no biggie to purchase breakfast and espresso consistently. In any case, we should take a gander at exactly how much that is truly setting you back. You'll regularly spend something like $30 for only one full week of lattes—that is $120 every month! How else might you, at some point, manage that cash?

Due to the power of compounding money, if you continually deposit $120 into a venture account over an extended period of time, your coffee asset might increase in value to more than $10,000. You're drinking throughout the entire semester that your kids are in school!

Let's say you had a longer perspective and made a $120 monthly contribution for a while. Your cash reserves for lattes may rise to more than $55,000.

Additionally, assuming you have been contributing your investing funds for a considerable amount of time, your coffee money might grow to be more than $300,000. A daily latte or about a fourth of a million dollars? You see, I enjoy a good cup of coffee, but not so much.

Consider what small (or large) penances you can do right now if you want to put yourself in a position to be financially comfortable. Your future will be impacted by the routine actions you take today with your money.

Setting goals will help you achieve them.

Financial goals will have a big impact on your attitude, your tendencies, and finally, your life. When you are careful with every dollar you have, you are prepared to make your money go further. That means you get to complete more of the tasks you believe you should complete and develop plans for the tasks you will complete moving forward.

You can achieve more than you ever imagined, but you'll need a few financial goals to help you get there. Decide what you believe your future should look like, then decide what you want to do today to start it off.
You can choose to live by your terms as opposed to the bank's.
You can evade responsibility one final time.
You can establish financial security and spend money on things that are important to you.

There are several factors that affect how you present your financial goals, including examples include your upbringing, sources of inspiration, and personal future aspirations. Look at my

book, Know Yourself, Know Your Cash, to better understand why you handle money the way you do and what you can do to change it. In order to help you take control of your money and reach your financial goals more quickly, it goes to the root of your unique spending habits.
Remember that everything starts with a financial strategy as well. The business is located here. The setup is the problem.

Additionally, it has to do with how you manage your money carefully. Feel free to start your free, every-dollar budget today. Then, start executing those five steps to map out and reach your financial goals. No matter the time of year, you may make your desires come true. Get it now!

CONCLUSION

The Power of Action

All through this book, you've acquired information as well as procured the force of activity. Monetary supportability is definitely not an inactive state; it's a result of intentional decisions and steady endeavors. As you execute the standards and steps framed in this book, you'll observe a change in your monetary life. Here is a recap of the key moves you've made:

You've changed your cash mentality by restricting convictions and embracing overflow.

You've dominated planning nuts and bolts, making a reasonable spending plan that lines up with your objectives.

You've investigated the universe of the venture, enhanced your portfolio, and bridled the force of progressive accrual.

You've helped your pay through different systems, opening new monetary doors.

You've made a customized monetary guide, charting a course toward independence from the rat race.

The Proceeding with Excursion

Your journey to independence from the rat race doesn't end here; it's a continuous experience loaded up with development and potential open doors. Here are a few fundamental standards to convey to you as you proceed with your monetary excursion:

Guideline 1: Consistency is Vital

Consistency in your monetary propensities is a little-known technique. Keep on planning, saving, contributing, and looking for open doors for money development reliably. Little, trained activities over the long haul yield momentous outcomes.

Guideline 2: Adjust and Advance

The monetary scene is constantly evolving. Remain versatile and open to novel thoughts and valuable open doors. As your life conditions advance, change your monetary arrangement in a like manner.

Guideline 3: Look for Information

Information is your most important resource in the realm of money. Remain informed about venture markets, monetary patterns, and monetary procedures. The more you learn, the better prepared you are to pursue informed choices.

Guideline 4: Look for Proficient Exhortation

Perceive the worth of expert direction. Monetary counsels, bookkeepers, and expense experts can give master guidance and assist you with exploring complex monetary choices.

Guideline 5: Offer in return and share

As you achieve monetary completeness, consider rewarding your local area or causes you care about. Sharing your insight and assets can have a positive effect beyond your own monetary objectives.

You've left on this excursion sincerely, and you're furnished with the information and devices expected to succeed. Recall that monetary completeness isn't just about numbers; it's tied in with adjusting your monetary decisions to your qualities, desires, and the existence you need to lead.

As you step into the world with recently discovered monetary certainty, realize that the way to independence from the rat race is special for every person. Your process might have its exciting bends in the road; however, with the standards and steps framed in this book, you have a dependable manual to explore the intricacies of money.

Embrace your monetary guide with energy and goals. It's not just about accomplishing an objective; it's tied in with embracing a daily existence where you have the ability to settle on decisions that give you pleasure, satisfaction, and true serenity. "Be Financially Responsible: Five Simple Financial Roadmaps for Sustainable Life." is inside your span, and the excursion is yours to cherish. In this way, make your next stride with certainty, and may your financial future be loaded up with flourishing, overflow, and the acknowledgment of your fantasies.